Poetry and poetic language can c   that elude communication in other ways. The poems do just that, powerfully capturing both the pain of addiction and the hope of recovery. This book is highly recommended reading for anyone interested in working to facilitate change in the lives of those affected by substance misuse.

Justin Lincoln, PsyD
Psychologist, Peaks Recovery Centers

"In a dark time," wrote the poet Theodore Roethke, "the eye begins to see." These paeans to personal suffering and transformation born of addiction are themselves born of the hearts and minds of compatriots. This concise and lovely volume is a welcome offering from the literary fringes of our field—impassioned rejoinder to the normative channels of stimulus and response and the scholastic monotony that drove poor Nietzsche mad. Also moving is the overall aesthetic of the design and layout, a thing of refinement in itself. "Tragedy enlightens," pondered Arthur Miller once upon a time . . .

Ed Mendelowitz, PhD
Faculty, Saybrook University, Oakland, CA

All readers, regardless of their knowledge of addictions, can appreciate the authentic and creative voice in which the authors speak. This book is a prolific expression of the pain and suffering often connected to addictions, recovery, and relapse. The authors have used the "healing power of poetry" to provide readers with a mental model into the complexities involved in the world of addictions. This book offers hope and life through an "age old" method—the art of poetry.

Tiko Hardy LSW, PsyD
Newman University

Silent Screams: Poetic Journey Through Addiction and Recovery is a breathtaking collection of poems that traces the journey through the pain and resiliency found in people who experience addiction and discover a new lifelong mission of recovery. This book is highly recommended for anyone who seeks firsthand experience into the minds and souls of people in recovery. The poems contained within these pages add depth like no other has done. The reader's mind is filled with vivid images that evoke what it feels like to be in the deepest parts of active addiction. The contrast between pain and meaning shows others there is hope and change is possible. *Silent Screams* portrays the human side of addiction and recovery for a world needing most to hear this message.

Michael J. Gargano, MSEd
Counselor, Loyola Recovery Foundation.

With compassion and vision, Granger and Hoffman are able to poetically capture the journey of many affected by addiction and recovery. "Covered in oil, feeling drained, attempting to lift my wings and fly away, my oil has been washed away and I can take off my mask." The poetic journeys, so eloquently reminded me of places where my vision was lost and restored. This reading reminded me of visions and energy that restored my life. "The human capacity for strength and resilience has been captured, my mask will remain off."

Lesia Wortham, BA, CACII- Certified Addiction Counselor II
Recovery Unlimited LLC

Silent Screams:

Poetic Journeys Through Addiction and Recovery

By

Nathaniel Granger, Jr.

&

Louis Hoffman

University
PROFESSORS PRESS

Colorado Springs, CO
www.universityprofessorspress.com

First published in 2017. University Professors Press. United States.

ISBN 10: 1-939686-22-9
ISBN 13: 978-1-939686-22-0

University Professors Press
Colorado Springs, CO
www.universityprofessorspress.com

Front Photo by Richard Bargdill
Cover Design by Laura Ross

Dedication

For Anthony L. "Tony" Artis, my late friend, who stretched my personal boundaries (and patience) enough to allow me to embrace life and all that it entails. Throughout the journey of addiction, recovery, relapse, etc., he stressed that in life less is often more, with drug addiction being no exception. "One is never enough and ten is too many," he would often say. Thank you, Tony, for your encouragement and the cherished gift of your friendship. R.I.P. Until we meet on the moon. — NG

For Brittany Garrett-Bowser, my good friend, who was the first person to deeply encourage me with my poetry and writing. Without your support, I am not sure I would have found the courage to pursue writing, which has become a vital part of my life and happiness. Thank you always for your encouragement, support, and, most important, your friendship. — LH

Poetry, Healing, and Growth Series

Stay Awhile: Poetic Narratives on Multiculturalism and Diversity
Louis Hoffman & Nathaniel Granger, Jr. (Eds.)

Capturing Shadows: Poetic Encounters Along the Path of Grief and Loss
Louis Hoffman & Michael Moats (Eds.)

Journey of the Wounded Soul: Poetic Companions for Spiritual Struggles
Louis Hoffman & Steve Fehl (Eds.)

Our Last Walk: Using Poetry for Grieving and Remembering Our Pets
Louis Hoffman, Michael Moats, and Tom Greening (Eds.)

Poems For and About Elders (Revised & Expanded Edition)
Tom Greening

Connoisseurs of Suffering: Poetry for the Journey to Meaning
Jason Dias & Louis Hoffman (Eds.)

Poetry, Healing, and Growth Series

The ancient healing art of poetry has been used across cultures for thousands of years. In the Poetry, Healing, and Growth book series, the healing and growth-facilitating nature of poetry is explored in depth through books of poetry and scholarship, as well as through practical guides on how to use poetry in the service of healing and growth. Poetry written with an intention to transform suffering into an artistic encounter is often different in process and style from poetry written for art's sake. This series offers engagement with the poetic greats and literary approaches to poetry while also embracing the beauty of fresh, poetic starts and encouraging readers to embark upon their own journey with poetry. Whether you are an advanced poet, avid consumer, or novice to poetry, we are confident you will find something to inspire your thinking on your personal path toward healing and growth.

Series Editors,
Carol Barrett, PhD; Steve Fehl, PsyD; Nathaniel Granger, Jr., PsyD; Tom Greening, PhD; and Louis Hoffman, PhD

Table of Contents

Acknowledgments

First, we would like to thank the many wonderful contributors who shared their hearts and their poetry with us. We also thank the many clients, students, friends, and acquaintances who have shared their stories with us over the years. The impact of these stories helped inspire *Silent Screams*. We would like to thank Laura Gundy for agreeing to write a Foreword, and Gary Forrest, for writing a Preface.

Nathaniel would like to express his heartfelt gratitude to his family—Areta, Nathan, Stephen, and Aliya—who have remained my biggest support and constant fan-base. Like other books in this series, the completing of this volume removed the scab from some old wounds, leaving them open to heal—and that's a good thing. In addition to my family, I would be remiss not to acknowledge the following people who have served as the salve of encouragement to ease the dissuasive sting of open wounds along this enigmatic journey: Louis Hoffman, Michael Moats, Richard Bargdill, Shawn Rubin, Krishna Kumar, Kirk Schneider, and Delaquaze Herbert, whose lasting friendship consisting of the good, bad, and ugly has served as a determinant to facing life's many challenges.

Louis first and foremost would like to thank his family—Heatherlyn, Lakoda, Lukaya, and Lyon—who lovingly support my addiction to writing and editing books! Anyone who has put together an edited volume like this knows the pain, joy, and time that it takes to complete such a volume. I wish to acknowledge the following people who have consistently supported me in my writing: Brittany Garrett-Bowser, Robert J. Murney, Theopia Jackson, Michael Moats, Nathaniel Granger, Jr., Ruth Richards, Glen Moriarty, Shawn Rubin, Richard Bargdill, John Hoffman, Joy Hoffman, Lynn Hoffman, and Clarence Hoffman.

Foreword

"I stand here feeling immobilized without options. Darkness surrounds me as I look forward, backward, and sideways. Am I alone in this? Does anyone know how I feel? Is there any possibility of happiness? Is there any hope for a life different than what I am experiencing? Death of the soul. Death of self." This statement is one felt by many who have had the experience of addiction. Addiction is powerful and has robbed the lives of so many who are affected by it. Those who suffer from the addiction and those who love the addict are both equally tormented by the crashing tidal waves of chaos and pain.

Silence Screams: Poetic Journeys Through Addiction and Recovery is a riveting collection of poems that bring to life the true experiences of men and women. As you move through the pages of this book, you will be taken into a day in the life of an addict and the aftermath of destruction left for those who love the addict. It will take you on a powerful journey of pain and hope.

In the moments of addiction, it is easy to fear that you are the only one. It is so easy to think that this is something not acceptable to talk about. Dr. Nathaniel Granger, Jr. and Dr. Louis Hoffman have orchestrated an inspiring gathering of works that open this conversation. It is hard to discuss the demons of addiction. How does one talk about a spouse who chooses the bottle over his children? How does one share the dark thoughts that arise when in a drunken episode? The stories brought to life in this book shed light on the deepest, darkest places that many have gone. Some have made their way back out, and, sadly, some have not. The poems offer a place of healing for those who may feel that no one understands.

As I read through the personal encounters so artfully captured in this book, I am brought to tears at the courageous honesty of the authors. Too many wonderful men and women have lost their lives due to the bottle or the drug. May the stories brought to life in this book help to show that addiction is not something to shame. There is freedom from addiction. Through the stories of others, we can find support when we feel alone. Together we can find moments of light in a world that can feel full of darkness.

Laura A. Gundy, PsyD

Preface

The editors of this text, Drs. Nathaniel Granger, Jr. and Louis Hoffman, and a cast of some fifty "poets" have constructed an excellent book of original poems that specifically focus on the experiences of people manifesting the spectrum of addictive disorders, as well as the families, friends, and loving people who have also been impacted by the addictive disease process. It should be noted in this context that contemporary science now refers to addictions as a "brain disease."

This little book unwittingly touches upon the long-recognized but often overlooked healing facets of the human expression of words, discourse, and relationship. Authors, "wordsmiths," and people who manifest a diversity of creative gifts seem to manifest a particular penchant for or susceptibility to the development of various patterns of addictive behavior. Authors such as Hemmingway, Fitzgerald, and Vonnegut, and musicians, actors, sport figures, great painters, gifted academics, physicians, and other creative groups seem to be over-represented in the mix of people manifesting the spectrum of addictive disease. These individuals also tend to be highly sensitive, bright, articulate, and insightful in many arenas of life; however, they may be self-scotomizing in other arenas—particularly in the realm of their active addictive disease process. Yet, many of these individuals do recover via a myriad of ways. I have observed and repetitively experienced over the course of 45 years of clinical practice work specific to addictions that the healing impact of sharing, openness, authenticity and honestly, and genuine human relatedness via "therapeutic words," personal dialogue, and the intimate process of therapy—the *poetry* of hours of "therapeutic work" within the alliance framework—can be an incredible catalyst for change and recovery. In this context, recovery-focused poems represent another "royal road to recovery" for many persons who struggle with addiction.

From the editors' introduction of this text, to the purpose and general clinical information that is touched upon early in the book, and each of the poems included in this work, addictive-disordered persons in recovery and those who may remain, along with those who love them, in the "addictive trap" will be confronted with bits and pieces of the experiential reality associated with their personal histories related to the addictive disease process.

I would definitely recommend this book as a helpful and viable tool for recovering individuals, the significant others in their lives, and treatment providers. Many of the poems in this work unmask the internal dynamics of shame, guilt, remorse, depression, compulsion and obsession, relapse, sexuality and acting-out, self-defeating behavior, and all that eventually comes to be in the course of the addictive disease process. These poems also reflect insight, growth and change, humor, joy, as well as the reflections associated with recovery and "rebirth." This book will also be a good resource for addictions counselors, educators, and patients. On a more personal note, as I read several of the poems in this work, I very quickly found myself wanting to make this book available to some of my current patients—angry patients, patients dealing with sexual trauma, family-of-origin issues, entitlement and narcissism, acting-out, self-defeating behavior. This text addresses a myriad of issues and dynamics related to the addictive disorders and behavioral health problems of many, many people.

Individuals and families in early-stage recovery may struggle with the content and harsh realities associated with the personal reflections that can be triggered by some of these poems. Sharing these feelings and dynamics with therapists, sponsors, or recovery support groups may foster a continued recovery process, and divert further relapses, vicarious traumatization experiences, or alliance ruptures.

Gary G. Forrest, EdD, PhD
Licensed Clinical Psychologist and Executive Director
Psychotherapy Associates, P.C., Colorado Springs, CO)

Introduction

Piss in a cup and drink it everyday and you will know the mental compromises it takes to be an addict. ~Sarge

As humans, we are creatures of habit. When bathing, we wash our bodies habitually—lather, wash under the left arm first with right hand, then under the right arm with left hand, private areas, face, etc., albeit maybe not in that order. Try switching the order in which you wash your different body parts, and you will find that going contrary to your norm may throw a monkey wrench into your morning! Our methodology of bathing, eating, drinking, sex, and other parts of our routine become routine because it feels "right" initially; it's pleasurable at first but later simply becomes a habit, our modus operandi.

Addiction is a habit gone awry, and many people are living with an addiction of some sort. According to the American Society of Addictive Medicine:

> Addiction is characterized by inability to consistently abstain, impairment in behavioral control, craving, diminished recognition of significant problems with one's behaviors and interpersonal relationships, and a dysfunctional emotional response. Like other chronic psychological problems, addiction often involves cycles of relapse and remission. Without treatment or engagement in recovery activities, addiction is progressive and can result in disability or premature death. (para. 2)

Addiction is more than a simple behavioral problem. Even when not based on substance use, addiction impacts the brain's functioning and the whole person.

I (Nathaniel) am fortunate not to have been born with Fetal Alcohol Syndrome—a term used for a range of disorders that include problems with vision, hearing, memory, attention span, and abilities to learn and communicate caused by drinking alcohol during pregnancy—in that my teenage mother was not to become plagued with the addiction to alcohol until years later. Nevertheless, by the time I left kindergarten to begin first grade in a public school on Chicago's South Side, I was already primed for an addiction or three. Legend has it that our parents put wine in our baby bottles so that we would go to sleep. How vivid the memory of the burn my three-year-old chest felt from the sip of my dad's whiskey and the inducement that it would put hair on my chest, thus morphing me into a man. Early mornings were filled with love as the smells emanating from Grandma's kitchen gently awakened me, with cigarette smoke, coffee, bacon, and pancakes ushering in the joy of a new day. Saturday morning cartoons were interrupted by commercials featuring the Marlboro Man, a suave cowboy puffing a filtered cigarette while riding through nature on a white stallion. In the evening, the bathroom reeking of marijuana was most comforting as it whispered, "Daddy's home." By the time I was 13, I met the criteria of an addict.

As with most pathologies, addiction begs the question of its etiology and effects—of whether it is nature or nurture. Genetic factors account for about half of the likelihood that an individual will develop addiction, whereas environmental factors interact with the person's biology and affect the extent to which genetic factors exert their influence. In other words, while there may be a genetic predisposition, the research does not support the assertion that addiction is genetic destiny. Resiliencies the individual acquires through parenting, later life experiences, and relationships can affect the extent to which genetic predispositions influence the behavioral and other manifestations of addiction. Culture also plays an important role in how addiction becomes actualized in persons with biological vulnerabilities to the development of addiction.

Addiction can impact every sphere of one's life including family relationships, friendships, work, hobbies, physical health, and more. Addiction, too, impacts various aspects of one's brain, including impairment of impulse control and judgment. Even one's spirituality can be deeply impacted by addiction.

Addictions steal the mind, body, and spirit; they take away one's voice! Recovery from addiction is often achieved through a combination of self-management, mutual support, and professional care provided by trained and certified professionals; however, each person's path to recovery is unique. Paramount in the therapeutic process on the road to recovery is the reclaiming of one's voice—having one's shared story heard. More often, the life and the story of those affected and infected by addiction is unheard—their song unsung.

The Journey of Addiction

Addiction is a beautiful lie. Recovery is an ugly truth.
~ Attributed to "M"

The TV Program "Unsung"—a documentary series that looks at some of the top R&B and soul artists of the last several decades, many of whom are not household names—features interviews with people who know the musicians well enough to describe the ups and downs of their careers. In watching episodes from this series, I (Nathaniel) found addiction to be a common nemesis that antagonizes stardom—the thing that dulls the luminosity of the star and, in many cases, fells the once shooting star. Individual episodes usually start with the story of an artist's upbringing, often depicting a rags-to-riches biography before delving into the trials and tribulations associated with stardom. The pinnacle of the performer's career plays out before a turning point that led to the beginning of a downward trend. The most common theme noted throughout the various episodes of lives of such artists as Ike Turner, Ray Charles, Rick James, and Tyrone Davis is the precipitating factor leading to their unsung status: Addiction.

No one is safe from addiction. While one can build resiliencies and protections against them, and some individuals are less prone to addiction than others, today's society seems replete with various forms of addition that range from drugs and alcohol to sex and internet addictions. For others, it may be a shopping or exercise or gaming addiction. Increasingly, it seems that almost everyone has their addiction. While some addictions may be more disruptive than others, any addiction has the ability to dislodge someone from their center and carry them on a journey over which they seem to have no control.

Often there is a shared quality to addiction. The poem "Buying Gum at 2:30" contains a story familiar to many in the throes of addiction to *the pursuit*—the story of how every day culminates in that anxiety-ridden 2:30 AM purchasing of gum just to get the cash back to continue the pursuit.

In the short poem "Vials," Bargdill speaks of the other ever-present pursuit of many struggling with addiction: the existential pursuit of something meaningful, something to fill the void and save the soul. For many struggling with addiction, not to be in pursuit of something is terrifying. Sitting or standing still is just too much to take until the pursuit momentarily is halted by the object of the addiction. But this is always a temporary pause until the pursuit resumes once again. It is a search to fill the existential void by obtaining the substance that numbs this void.

The Journey with Addiction

The pain of addiction is not reserved for the person caught in the thorns of addiction. Friends and loved ones suffer, too, as they watch the person they love fade into the addiction and slowly seem to become someone else—someone part the person they knew and someone part controlled by something outside themselves. For some, the title of Seluja's poem "Telephone, 4 a.m." is enough to give them shivers. The late night calls and texts and emails all represent a cry for help from a pit of suffering that seems beyond one's reach.

In "Dinner with the Demon," Lockie speaks to the first meeting with the external force that has taken over her loved one. For those who have not experienced such a meeting, it is hard to describe the horror of seeing someone else in the shell of a loved one—knowing that somewhere hidden beneath layers of pain the loved one still exists. Lockie writes,

> So I stroke the hand across from me
> with my stretched heart
> Only to understand the demon
> Has deadened it to my touch

These words show the powerlessness that one can feel when a loved one is caught in addiction. Though it is known that the loved one resides somewhere inside this shell, it seems impossible to reach them.

For the caregivers and loved ones of the person struggling with addiction, the question of "What should I do?" is ever-present. The "experts" will say "keep good boundaries" and "don't enable," and maybe even "they have to hit rock bottom before they can be saved." This new language may, at times, offer hope, but it does little to ease the suffering and offers no guarantee of success. The techniques are not easy, either. When a loved one is hurting, the impulse is to love more. In the last line of Carroll's poem "The First Night of My Son's Rehab," she simply asks, "what could I do but let him in?"

No amount of books, therapists, or meetings can provide a definitive answer on what, if anything will save the person caught in the throes of addiction. Even if every bit of advice is followed perfectly, there is no guarantee of success. As expressed in the poem "How to Love You,"

> how can anyone know how to love
> when eyes glaze over
> after the demons have taken hold
> when you know the one you love
> is slowly being strangled away

For the loved one, guilt becomes a constant companion and prompter of second-guessing. One wonders, "If only I had done this, then maybe..." These maybes can linger endlessly. The journey with addiction can be as lonely and isolating as the journey through addiction. Friends do not understand or do not know how to help. Sometimes fears of judgment and shame prevent one from reaching out for support. For those isolated and alone, we hope these poems may be one source of comfort and knowledge that you are not alone.

Purpose of this Book

To find peace, you have to be willing to lose your connection with the people, places, and things that create all the noise in your life. ~unknown

We have organized the poems in this book into two sections: Journeying Through, which represents the experience of people with addictions, and Journeying With, which represents the experience of friends and loved ones that have shared the journey of addiction through their love and concern for the person struggling with addiction. Poems are always challenging to classify and some poems could fit in either section.

Writing, and particularly sharing writing on addiction, is challenging. Often, there is shame connected with addiction for the addict as well as for family and friends. For many, it is easier to talk about depression, anxiety, fears, or other psychological difficulties than to address the addiction itself. Each poem in *Silent Screams* can be understood as an act of courage. We hope that by reading these poems others are empowered to write about and share their own journeys through and with addiction. For those still struggling with the addiction, we hope reading these poems and being inspired to write one's own poems may become a source of strength to journey through the addiction to recovery.

The purpose of this book is not to glorify addictions but to give voice to the addict, the addiction, those impacted by the addict's addiction, and, in some cases, the object of addiction. As with other books in the Poetry, Healing, and Growth Series, this is achieved through poetic narratives that give voice to the experience—in this case, the journey through and recovery from addictions. The "voices" contained in this volume, along with various art forms, were purposely included with the resolute goal that the reader will gain a greater sense of empathy for the addict and those impacted by the behaviors of those struggling with addiction. In addition, our aim is that the reader will also gain a greater understanding of addictions' various forms. The *power* of these vices, and the respective intricacies associated with obtaining, using, living with, and ultimately overcoming the "drug" of choice. In fact, the power of external cues to trigger craving and drug use, as well as to increase the frequency of engagement in other potentially addictive behaviors, is also a characteristic of addiction: The hippocampus is important in the memory of previous euphoric or dysphoric experiences, and the amygdala is important in directing motivation to concentrate on selecting behaviors associated with these past experiences. Although some believe that the difference between those who have addiction and those who do not is the quantity or frequency of alcohol/drug use, engagement in addictive behaviors (such as gambling or spending), or exposure to other external rewards (such as food or sex), a characteristic aspect of addiction is the qualitative way in which the individual responds to such exposures, stressors, and environmental cues.

A particularly pathological aspect of the way that persons with addiction pursue substance use or external rewards is the persistent preoccupation with, obsession with, and/or pursuit of rewards (e.g., alcohol and other drug use) despite the accumulation of adverse consequences. These manifestations can occur compulsively or impulsively, as a reflection of impaired control. Hence, a disclaimer: The stories depicted here elicit some very strong emotions—sorrow, regret, anger, grief, shame, guilt, contempt, joy, and laughter. Some poems within this volume, unintentional of their authors, may trigger cravings and/or other physiological manifestations. Following the initial reaction, the chief aim is that hope is realized in every person dealing with an addiction—that every seemingly unsung voice crying out from the soul of every person experiencing an addiction will resound like a clarion call that allows all to hear your *Silent Screams*.

References

American Society of Addictive Medicine (2011). Public policy statement: Short definition of addiction. Retrieved from http://www.asam.org/docs/default-source/public-policy-statements/1definition_of_addiction_short_4-11.pdf?sfvrsn=0

Poems:
Journey Through

Why Maury and I Go To The Methadone Clinic Book Club

Sarah Shotland

Because it doesn't take much movement to read.
Because there are free paperbacks at stake.
Because sometimes we need to be in a room with each other
and not be expected to talk about hope or gratitude,
but just a book, and its rotten characters,
its shitty setting.
Because we want to be reminded that, yes,
page 122 claims the love-torn couple have ridden the train from
   Atlanta
to Sacramento,
but we know better than to believe anything really changes.

Because we are convinced, every Tuesday,
from 10:00-11:30 a.m. that we are more
than our half dozen varieties of fuck up.
We are the stuff of literature.
Sometimes we choose the low-hanging
fruit: Bukowski and Burroughs. People enjoy Neil Gaiman and who
   can blame them.
But one month, the new woman on 220 mg.
says she's always wanted to read Jane Austen
and Maury says
who gives a fuck, they'll be the same kind of rotten as the rest.
And so we read, the six of us, *Pride and Prejudice.*

This is a book club where everyone claims to be ten years younger
   than their tattoos.
Where everyone's first drink was a year ago.
Where we are all waiting for a great denouement,
a perfect untangling,
a fabulous re-enactment of our own undoing.
Here we are, Maury and I,
syrup caught between our teeth,
pretending to talk at the exposition
of longing. Pretending there is something in the backstory beyond

the shape of our mouths agape.
Because, for that hour and a half a week,
it is the writers who remind us that we are no worse or better
than Mr. Darcy and Ms. Bennet,
that we're just like all the other babies whose mouths were born
crying that same shape of more.

Trying to Be Alcoholic
Ann Cefola

I order another plum wine, the small goblet
like a purple crocus whose blossoms burn.
I want to taste the tree of spiked knowledge,
that fermented fruit which entranced my parents.

On my second glass, air turns liquid, restaurant aquarium.
I am a gourami mouthing syllables with difficulty.
My head, loose seaweed, sways in the current.
Surely this shell will yield the pearl.

After my first few drinks, I give up trying to relate.
I acknowledge the half-eaten apple, snickering snake.
Where to find the gardener who assigned my parents
their unquenchable fate — someone supremely unwise

who showed them you can't consume a garden
but, over and over, you can drink paradise.

"Trying to Be Alcoholic" originally appeared in *Natural Bridge,* Spring 2003.
Reprinted with permission.

Observed by Sparrows

Cynthia Rosi

On a Boston park bench
beside the stone angel
sits a young woman
without a song to throw a cloak
over her.

Bricks and mortar of friendship
are experiences and affection.
Loneliness yearns to breach the wall.

A man approaches
begging for cigarettes.
He reaches a palm toward her.
A bud of blood
domes against his wrist

and she stretches young woman's fingers
to him, brushing away the crimson bead
as gently as his mother would,
as she who will greet him in the hour
of his death.

As her innocence unfurled,
she forgot to pull down her sleeves.
Tiny lies
ladder her arms.

Smooth eyes of the stone angel
blind to you,
but carved to see.

Observed by Sparrows, Response
Artist, Sofia Rosi

Buying Gum at 2:30
Nathaniel Granger, Jr.

We first took off
around a quarter till 10
stopping at the Liquidy-Q
for a six-pack of Colt 45
and a rose, and a single
not-for-individual-resale
wad of Brillo
Illegal, but who's tellin'

The tiny rose encased in the glass tube
Usually ignored, sits on my dash
while he fixes the glass stem
with the copper scouring
Our little good-luck charm
To ward against them coming
Is soon forgotten
At the first blast from the past

Mouth salivates,
stomach cramps
The twenty dollars cash-back
Hurls into motion the night
We run here, then there
Down the alley, on the left
A double-up for coming correct with an extra 5
and a promise to come again

The ear-ringer! The chase!
Battery dead or phone ignored
Except for the text, "Come through"
The stores closed, even the Liquidy-Q,
Code for Liquor Store,
In the event we have to hook-up there
But the house down the alley on the left is still up
No cash, nor chain to barter

Tweaking, sweating
With dilated pupils
Gaining composure
As the automatic doors usher us in
Trapping us as they slide shut behind us
The cashier knows...
It's 2:30 in the morning
At the Wal-Mart checkout
Lane 4 again
A pack of gum rests on the conveyor
As the debit card pin is typed
Praying it's not declined
I get twenty dollars cash-back
Snatch the gum
And escape quickly for one more
Into the overdrawn morning.

Vials
Richard Bargdill

I
couldn't
save my
soul
In a
thousand
vials

Tempest (Photo) by Richard Bargdill

Clouds
Nathaniel Granger, Jr.

Response to (photo) by Richard Bargdill

Blotched plumes fluff
Painted puffs
Under one canopy blue
The World's Biggest Circus—
Elephants, clowns,
The taming of a shrew
The face of Jesus dissipates
Then morphs into something else.

Cottony clouds
Billow proud
Above my head on high
Humbly dive to fill my core
Lungs trying
The exhale not shy
Release them to their ascent
To morph into something else.

The Bar

Jon Vreeland

She smiled at me when I sat down.
What a woman,
The type you find in a dream.
She was sitting at the bar
sipping her drink,
ignoring everyone in the room.
She was much too beautiful for them;
Sloths
Reeking of gin,
cheap cigars,
the bottle with the old sailor ship;
business men who had told their wives

"hey I'm working."

Yeah,
It was one of those days;
But it was a Tuesday
and nobody felt like working
just to remain in debt.

(Your phone will still scream at 6am!!
Leeches to suck you dry!!)

They were there to forget their lives
wives
kids
work
god
etc.
But only for a while.
I ordered another drink and
went into the bathroom to fix.
When I returned to the bar her smile had vanished
(Vanished only when she looked at me)
She glanced down at my left arm,
then walked out of

The Bar
Leaving her glass half full
and a cigarette dying
in the turquoise marble ashtray.

No Sympathies for a City
Richard Bargdill

The last night in a city
I don't want fond memories of.
The last night of drinking alone
In a bar full of people.

Today I could not climb out of my coffin
And ask about her sign
Which inevitably said "STOP."
Even the weather was too stable
To talk about.
The sports team lost again today
And I drank again today
And was only temporarily bothered by ideas of health
That might come outside the city
Only temporarily bothered by the gray winds of sentimentalism
Which have no ground in my sky
Only temporarily bothered
Between sips.

I leave this city
just like my last night here
Detached.
Flying away like a single seed
Of a flowered dandelion
That some kid has kicked
Kicked for the fun of it
Kicked for the boredom
Kicked because it got in the way
Of his meandering.
Floating, not flying, rudderless
A miracle of evolution:
A weed/seed
Carried like a lone paratroop
Hoping to land in the yards
Not sprayed with chemicals
Hoping not to land on the concrete
Hoping not to land in the rushing river of busyness

Hoping to land on fertile ground
And do what weeds do
Grow
And make others think about
How ugly we are.

Gold Tipped Feathers Hanging from the Heavens

Gina Subia Belton

Dedicated to Dr. Joseph Giovannetti

"Contract suicide"
spoke the Tolowa Elder
"they never had a chance,"

The people who grew
"out of the land here like grass,"
generations lost.

Hopeless fulfillment
of toxic pathologies,
an unwelcomed accord

with perverse madness.
She said, "A ceremony"
a coyote dance

to break this contract
with the "new world" killing us.
Yes, generations lost,

you thought you buried
us but you only planted seeds.
Our resilience. . .

. . . will set us free.
We've buried enough young ones"
Others sway near the soil . . .

Dedicated

. . . To "contract suicide".
What we need is ceremony,
a coyote dance

. . . To set us FREE.
To remember, we stand on
the love of thousands.

A Letter from Me
Delaquaze Herbert

Dear addiction,

You have left me with many scars and bruises
At times, you've taken everything I love
You've taken my self-respect, my dignity
And many other things I don't care to mention
But there is a magical thing called recovery
It is your kryptonite
I will fight you with everything I have inside me
Not only will I fight,
I will win.

-A survivor

Animal
Amanda Stephan

I've untied my animal mask
retracted my claws.
My coat's been shed in clumps
irradiated with knowledge of self
no longer insulated by ignorance.
My animal self
dead-eyed and dormant
with all other extinct creatures.
The heat of thought
forced it from my flesh
stinking of sour sweat and
matted with evidence of violence.
I am naked in this newness
and awkwardly aware
swinging two left arms
attached to skill-less hands
not yet mature enough to grasp
not yet mature enough to hold without harm.

Milkshakes and Chilidogs

Bartholomew Barker

I enjoy many vices
They need not be cataloged here
Some of them are killing me
Slowly

I should quit
But I'm addicted
Neither nagging
Nor negotiation
Nor nutritional knowledge
Has stopped me
Driving thru
To my doom

I will regret my weakness
I already do
If I'm lucky
It will finish me quickly
No wasting away
Life draining through tubes
In antiseptic rooms

I want to die fat and happy
I want to meet my chiligod
With a milkshake in my hand

Downfall

Amanda Stephan

A spectacular downfall
This woman has stumbled
Out of and into herself
A version both tall and short
A version both strong and weak

Perhaps somewhere in the middle of all things.

A sleeping march
This woman has woke
And slept and woke again
To a world too loud with all the wrong things
To a world too quiet with soundless conversation

Perhaps somewhere in the middle of all things.

Vide Verre
Richard Bargdill

There is an emptiness inside of me
An emptiness I try to fill up
I try to fill it with everything I know
Now I am trying to fill it with poison
How can poison fill a hole?
Empty words come out of my full mouth
Fat ideas belch from my mind
But how can they rest on top of nothingness
Do I think I can kill the hole with explosives
Does everything have a leak
Where are the ear plugs, nose plugs, eye plugs
Call the ear wax repairman
With his shades, walkman, cigarettes, booze
You can lock yourself in
Beware though of fires
Because there's just enough of a leak
That the flames can be engulfing.
Then all there is left is a structure
Insides burnt out.

Crisis of the week has 31 flavors
And no one is ever happy
We all think our lives important enough
That we should be going through pain
I knew a possessed poet who thought
He had to suffer to be good.
Yeah, there's a number of walls around to
Bang your head through, pick one and
See if you make any progress
Because if you do then
Someone can tell you, you're right
And you can feel like a
Whore.

Dripping by Richard Bargdill

The Door
John E. Steele

I don't know how many days
or weeks
or years
I spent
In the darkness
looking for The Door,
The way out – the *real* way out.

I know every brick,
Every crack in the walls of my cell,
This tomb is of my own creation.

Staying awake, fighting the nightmare,
Fighting the creatures, emotions, who are my captors,

Until sleep
overtakes
me.

Oh, I took hostages, took them, held them, suffocated them...
Until they revolted....

and I
wondered
why

Confined within the endless corridors of my inner self.....
Searching!!
Ignoring the exits all the while wondering *which way is out?*

(The Door!)

Ignoring the truth of my existence,
Creating within a world believing that it was
The world outside as well.

Confusing myself, confining myself –

fooling ...
only ...

myself

Knowing now what I wouldn't believe then,
Knowing which way is out
The Door!!
in front of me
(Recovery!)

The thick, cold planks
sealed with cobwebs ....
Fear, the impasse!
Fear, the enslaver!
Fear, the Killer of Hope and Dreams!

Just to reach forward, outside myself,
Outside the walls of my cell,
To open, ever so slightly,
The Door.

Sunshine, light, blinds my mind's eye,
Blink, blink, blink.....
The pain of the light, burning into my flesh,
So long hidden in the darkness of shame, guilt, loneliness and pain
Yet....
Feeding my soul, killing the killer
Fear enslaving the feared, the fearful!

Wanting to be in the light,
Wanting to be free
From me
My own worst enemy.

Duel messages, duel confusion splattered by moments
Of clear thought, splattered by swelling tides
Of emotions of unknown origins,
From the shore of some distant dark forgotten shore,
From the rock strewn carnage of distant shores of the past.

Ancient bones beneath layers of debris and forgotten things,
Layers of soot, layers of organic rot – no!
Layers of the slow dying death that is, no,
That was my spiral.

So are the essences of my personhood
Buried beneath soot, and layers of time,
Wasted time, time spent wasted beneath tons of
Carnage created by the tornado
Of my being.

Fear encrusted, never dusted corridors
Of feelings, emotions — of the pure
Meaning behind being human.

As my buried soul rises from beneath the sands of time,
Slowly escaping the living tomb of my fear's creation,
Slowly standing, as I learn to steady myself, and walk
On wobbly, shaky legs......

.....through The Door

Anger

Amanda Stephan

Today I hold captive this tongue
notoriously quick to split and spit venom
because today in the silence of this battered brain
I heard a most reasonable voice
urging me
with sounds so soft and humble
to be thankful.

Be thankful that you feel this Anger
it said
because this means you are saved.
Turn it inside out in your mind
instead of hurling it against your Lover
or your Mother
or your Children.

Hold this Anger up like a map
that shows you where to find yourself-
where you've been
where you never want to go again
where your boundaries are
and give thanks.

These words were a foreign language
to this dumb child
and the stretch of silence before I spoke
was an unfamiliar region
but I stayed there
until through a cell of broken teeth
I heard my tongue move in thanks.

For Filo
Sarah Shotland

I met Filo
in the parking lot
of the Cesar Chavez Stop and Go,
where Jade told me,
girl, you're gonna meet a man
who'll let you lose all those other small time
shitbags. He'll give you that personal
number. Never make you wait.
He asked
you married,
my favorite pick up line of all,
because it didn't require a lie.

I told him I was a for-profit enterprise,
that everything in the world was for sale.
I told him his daughter was lucky
to have a daddy who bought her a purple Mustang to cruise the east
side.
I told him sure, I can do that too, I can do it all.
I told him he had the best dope in Austin,
but that was a lie.
It was just that he'd let me suck his cock to get it,
and after all, I had a college loan to pay back,
I couldn't be spending all that money on tar.

I told him of course, on your birthday
you don't pay for anything.
I told him, though, it's my birthday, too,
so I don't pay for anything either.
He thought that was funny—
and I liked it when Filo laughed.
I liked to see the back of his teeth,
thick like nickels
and nickel bags stuck between gums and tongue.
I liked to see the inside of his mouth caught up his throat.
I told him I was an independent contractor.
And when he would ask if I was okay,

I told him he wasn't paying to worry about my feelings.

More than his hand on my head around his cock,
Filo wanted to talk.
About the accomplishments of his daughter,
the troubles with his sister who stayed in the house he paid the
mortgage on.
He wanted to talk about the laundromat he fronted,
and the way his girlfriend couldn't make churros
the way his mother had, even though she tried,
even though she knew he wanted them tight like
spun corn fried in fat, thick straws of memory.
You have to own property one day, he told me.
I laughed,
but he shut my mouth,
said *with all the body I buy off you,
at least own a piece of something
to sit your sweet flat ass on.*

Filo came to me on lunch breaks
and in extended stay hotels,
he came to me in half hours and hour and a halves.
In parking lots is mostly where he came in my mouth.
Today, when people press their hands against my head,
I buck,
because they are no men like Filo.
I date men who ride the bus and think profit
is a dirtier word than anything
that could come out of my kind mouth.
I date men who punch in and out,
who come home tired.

The truth is, I am still a for-profit enterprise,
the way I give and withhold again,
say wait,
you don't get it all yet.
I work the scarcity side
of supply and demand now,
tease the nickels from my legs like
a tight fist.
Because the side that says scarcity

is the side that holds promise,
in all its longing.
The way a mouth will open slow,
and then wide,
hoping to be filled with the sweetness
of coins against a tongue.

Monday Morning
Eileen Malone

After a night of heavy drinking
I pull open the motel blackout curtains
to a pawned harbor town
where ships no longer come and go

all that I promised I would not do
I did last night with a part time bartender
younger than the age I was then

he delivered enough free drinks
to earn the fantasy and spasm
of sex with me, then the privilege
of departure while I'm passed out

he left behind a stench of sweat
an almost empty bottle of cheap whiskey
and his dirty white cigarette lighter

I flick it open, think pirates, stowaways
hold the flame to bed bugs
that pirouette from punched pillows
to my eyebrows

shut it just before burning my forehead

uncertain of what's coming next
knowing only that it's soon.

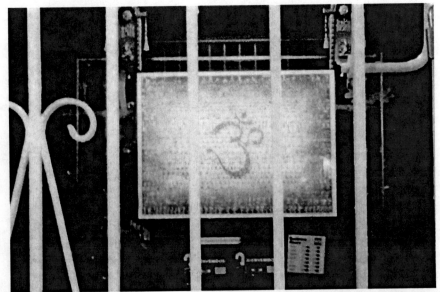

"Om Behind Bars" by Juliet Rohde Brown

Butterfly
Kelly Bargabos

Sloe Gin Fizz
bubbles in your mouth before it parties downward, seducing you with
promises. Beer fills you, settling in your gut the way a warm bowl of
chili might on a winter day. Light dispels the darkness. Warmth
dispels the cold. A salve to your wounds. Softens the sharp edges of
your mind, your soul. Whiskey burns as it goes down, its sweetness
you inhale, like sinking into bed after a cold day, like thick blankets,
holding you in a cocoon, walls holding you tight, in a safe, familiar
place. You know this place—let it take you to that night you were
thirteen, and sixteen, then twenty-three, now forty-five—transforming
you into a butterfly.

Butterflies
everywhere you look, everyone is a butterfly but you. On your belly
you scratch on the dusty hard ground, a caterpillar, wooly and prickly,
searching for the magic cocoon that will make you one of them.
Elegant shades of brown and gold. Pink and sapphire. Wings like
angels, wings iridescent, wings that glow, wings that fly you closer to
the sun, wings that take you where you dream of. Mesmerized by the
wine...*when it is red, when it sparkles in the cup.* The hope of it; the
dream of it—flapping in your mind until you drink it.

You fly
into the sun's fire, a slow burn starts, your colors begin to fade, your
wings move slower and slower, it takes you longer and longer to find
that magic cocoon until one day your wings fail and you land hard on
the dusty ground, on your belly. And the next time you try to fly you
fall.

When shall I awake, that I may seek another drink?

Wings break, tear,
each time you fall, another piece of you gone, soon there will be
nothing left. And then one day you crawl inside your bottle, but the
magic has died. You don't change, you can't fly. The cocoon that once
transformed you, gave you wings, now holds you prisoner and you,

having swallowed the key, are chained inside. Neither a caterpillar nor a butterfly.

Obsession

Andrea Potos

In darkness you leave your home
and walk miles to call him.
You stand in the cold of the phone booth;
iron hinges from the torn-off door
are like ice scraping at your back.

The phone burns in your hands.
The wind stings your fingertips and toes.
Sirens shriek past you on the street, your gaze trailing
the blaring red cones of light as if they were signals
to some destination you forgot.

You strain to hold his words
like polished stones you could hoard.
You forget rest and warmth for this night--
you possess an energy
you would never need if you were whole.

Fire Starter
Amanda Stephan

I'm an alcoholic.
Like any true alcoholic
I accept no absolutes
outside of the bottled variety.
Nothing is true without adequate testing
including the truth that I'm an alcoholic.

Each leaf of truth cast down
by those much taller and sturdier than I
has been crushed into a palatable consistency
to put in my pipe and smoke.

I have ground great piles of wisdom
into a coarse collection of words:
God and Goodness
Motherhood and Moderation
Wife and Work
and burned them.

So long I've sat lost in hazy firelight
exhaling only smoke and hot air
that I've forgotten the shape of my body and
my mind can't assemble all of the real I've dismantled.

I've become an edgeless form
unable to outline myself.

I want to be a woman
with soft curves and a sweet mouth.
I want to be a woman
with pillow-tipped fingers.
But first I must be a human
that doesn't always bind myself
into the saddle of discomfort
and ride off in search of things to set ablaze.

This is a truth that I hold a match to
this night and every night
as I consider whether or not to fill my glass.

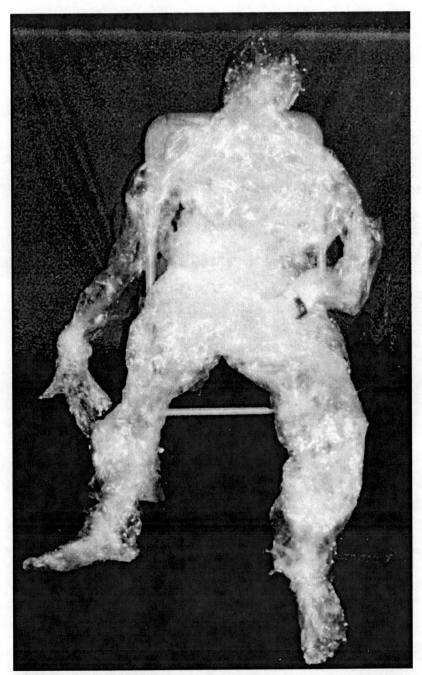

"Molted" by Richard Bargdill.

Some Other Me
Nathaniel Granger, Jr.

Inspired by the photograph "Molted" by Richard Bargdill

Please, do not stand aloof
by reason of the me
you now see

In your eyes you've distanced
but I need you close
Rescue me

My heart beats with yours
Yet, cannot connect
This can't be

For the one you loved
and now behold
has become some other me.

The Journey of Addiction
Damon Taylor

Addiction is a journey of lifeless searching,
Searching to be numb of the emotional bondage
of love as it is painfully known.
The lifeless journey of addiction
cost: the beauty of hope, joy, and peace
that the person in recovery would know.
The fear of facing the unknown
because the addiction has consumed
the identity of the addict
and has become the skill of coping,
coping with emotions, fears, anxiety, and depression.

Not knowing anything outside
of feeding that dark place
because it becomes the comfort zone of hopelessness.
The fear of recovery bleeds through the heart of the addict—
recovery means change
and facing the fear of feeling
those emotions that were once felt.
The fear of recovery rushes in
and all the thoughts of escaping the drudgery
of life in recovery
with all the peace, joy, and happiness that could be
if only I give myself a chance.

Why should I give myself a chance
this identity that addiction has
brings the lack of responsibility,
the lack of other's ability to trust
who I am and what my addiction will cause me to do,
the lack of being able to say to myself
I Love You and your worth is priceless,
the lack of feeling hopeful and not a delusion of hope,
the lack of acceptance of the world
as being what it is—a beautiful place filled with beautiful people,
the lack of knowing what tomorrow will bring
because I have prepared for it today,

and the lack of experiencing love
and not just being selfishly engaged in activities
to get my next high.

This journey has killed thousands
and ruined the lives of tens of thousands but I,
yes, I have to embrace healing
to escape the delusion of the painful journey of addiction.

In the Void
by Norman A. Magnus

"I call a lie: wanting *not* to see something one does see, wanting not to see something *as* one sees it... The most common lie is the lie one tells to oneself; lying to others is relatively the exception." ~ Nietzsche

The morning light enters the room—
a spotlight on my shame
The familiar rubbery smell
mixed with bodily fluids
sinks into my chest
I try to lie deadly still
The night before, barely passed,
already haunts my day
I recount my steps
searching for justification

"Just a drink. I'll go home alone."
A familiar sin
At a second drink the curves
begin enticing
drawing me closer. Then
the smell, the touch, the taste...
Back in her apartment
I pass the void in me
to the void in her

Escape fades in the emerging light
as the warmth against my back
comes to life
She lets out a morning moan
her hand slides over my chest
pulling me in, and I know
we dance differently with the void...
My momentary escape,
Was her hope for something more

Here I Stand

Geoffrey S. Browning

Thinking back to the time we had,
Here I stand.
Remembering feeling like a hundred grand,
Here I stand.

I was hurt from dishonesty,
The trouble I had found had haunted me.
When she came around, Lord, she set me free.

It was after I pushed her away,
That I would see. And convey.
Who she really was and what she had lent me.

Naturally astounding, and her love, a fantasy.
Punishing the boy, but unlocking the man in me.
After she left, with her keys in her hand.
She closed the door, leaving me to the land.

Here I stand.

Revelation
Delaquaze Herbert

Where I was one
Now there're two.

Silent Scream
Nathaniel Granger, Jr.

People laughing at the absurd—gunshots, sirens
Music pumping through house speakers
Eerily imitating the pounding in my chest
The bass beating the drum in my ear
And yet, most deafening
Is the sound of silence.

In its quietness I hear my name
Called only to offer just one more.
I answer,
Knowing that one is never enough
And ten is too many.
Again, I go there—
Nowhere in particular

I answer the phone—
The ringing only heard by my own ears
I close the blinds
To hide myself from the watchers watching,
The peepers peeping
While the tweakers tweak
And this sneaker sneaks
In hopes of muffling the silent scream.

But then, I drop a piece!
In desperation I comb the shag,
Picking their rug like my own 'fro
To find the piece I dropped
The piece of my imaginings
The piece of my mind
A piece of my dignity.

I am hungry but cannot eat
I eat but cannot swallow
I scream but cannot voice
The pain from within the abyss.
I'm trippin'—Falling, deeply even.

Shattered glass reflects like diamonds
The hours that have become days
The days, weeks
Weeks, months…
What's today's date, anyway?

Yesterday, a year ago
It was better than life.
Alas, today
It is worse than death
And no one,
No one but perhaps God
Will hear my silent scream.

Poems:
Journeying With

The First Night of My Son's Rehab
Judith Waller Carroll

One guilt-drenched dream
after another, till finally

near dawn, hope
in the form of a silver tabby,

half-starved and keening,
an entreaty so constant and pitiful,

what could I do but let him in?

"The First Night of My Son's Rehab" was originally published in *Clementine Unbound*. Reprinted with permission.

Empty
Jennifer Lagier

He used to take time
to hide the dead soldiers
before I got home,
mixed alcohol
with oxycodone,
marijuana, cocaine.
Didn't want to hear
lectures about his liver,
drunken tumbles,
missed work days.
Now he doesn't bother
to camouflage the vodka bottle
with bags of frozen vegetables,
too hard to find
after a handful of norcos,
two or three bottles of wine.
By midnight,
he's unresponsive,
video games blaring,
booze spilled on the carpet.
I check respiration, pulse,
my heart on empty,
wonder whether to
celebrate liberation
or dial 911.

"Empty" was previously published in the journal *Dead Snakes*. Reprinted with permission.

Vigil
Michael Coolen

I listen to the sound of my beautiful son breathing.
I watch his chest rise and fall,
I hear his breathing with the finely tuned
ears of a musician able to hear
one instrument in an orchestra playing the wrong note

I listen for wrong notes
I watch his chest with the eyes of a father
who watched his son sleep
long after he could walk
I hear troubling breaths
interrupted by even more troubling silences

I choose to keep listening
hoping his breath becomes regular
I choose to watch as his body twitches
a reaction to the drug he ingested
I choose to listen watch hear a little longer
knowing that a trip to the ER
is the same as trip to jail
where they will not listen or watch or hear
or help

I will stand vigil as I have stood vigil before
waiting hoping longing until...
there there there
there
the sound I have longed for
even regular at rest

I can stop listening for now
I can stop watching for now
I can stop worrying for now.

I can breathe again
for now

To My Brother

Sarah Cooper

You wanted to be cool like boys
who said "school" with bitter snarls

whose mouths mocked authority
who wanted to rob your life.

I watched you slip, slide and sail
down to the dip of detention,

read your rehab letters late
at night, ignored your pleading

phone calls. Boundaries we called it.
I heard your son refuse to say your name

watched your Atlantic eyes dry up.
We rested you in an oak casket

hands folded, eyelids glued
shut.

Dinner with the Demon
Ellaraine Lockie

Finally I meet his demon
Furtive creature descended
from the depths of his ancestry
Sitting across from me
stalking diners in the restaurant
through his alcohol-alert eyes
In the darting caged-fear way
that could make me stop frequenting zoos

His ogle eyes target others
who guzzle his fuel
The repairperson part of me
to the rescue with diversion
of World War II related dialogue
But my knowledge is nominal
As irritating to him
as the forty-five minute food wait

Our server has become
the demon's next visual victim
My dinner partner's fight to be polite
extracts another attempt from me to entertain
But I'm as inept at jokes
as I am about Hitler

So I stroke the hand across from me
with my stretched heart
Only to understand the demon
has deadened it to my touch
Dinner is delivered
just in time before he bolts
The demon disappears
And I begin to digest the discovery
that I'm as unable to help as is this man

How to Love You
Louis Hoffman

3 AM
whispers and laughter
followed by a quick screech of tires
float in my cracked window
I never fully sleep anymore
always listening for these sounds
hoping, tonight, maybe,
you'll make it through the doorway
or at least to the porch before the neighbors, too,
awake, and turn on the front lights

maybe you'll say you're sorry
maybe you'll promise to sober up
maybe you'll cry and put your head on my lap
maybe...

I grab my robe and for a moment
stare out the window at the saturated
mound of flesh and clothes in the front lawn
the grass is cold and wet with dew
gathered quickly by my robe
"let's go inside honey, sleep it off"
you try to help lift yourself from the ground
the weight on my shoulders nearly pulls me down
but we make it through the door
before you fall onto the soft couch
I roll you to your side
knowing too well how to keep you alive

From the worn chair across the room
I witness
your breathing uneasy
chocking you briefly awake
each time your breath stops

I guiltily contemplate freedom
Then when your chest rises again
I remember our love
and the children we raised

they say my love hurts you
and maybe they are right
each time I save you
it becomes easier to fall
but I still cannot leave you cold
and alone
in the unrelenting night
maybe my love is not that strong

how can anyone know how to love
when eyes glaze over
after the demons have taken hold
when you know the one you love
is slowly being strangled away

I pull my robe tight
and prepare the coffee and aspirin
for the morning
and return to my fretful sleep

"Knowing the Difference" by Juliet Rohde-Brown

Addict
M. S. Rooney

This man
who sits
across from me
shaking,
who seems to want
any harbor
but his own
at any cost
but his own,
was once
my husband's mother's
sweet baby boy,
my husband's closest
baby brother. But one
by one the spokes
broke. Now
he tries to wheel
through webs
that no longer
yield before him.
How
can this vast span
between us
be?

On Learning That My Daughter's Rapist Has Been Taught to Write a Poem
Katharyn Howd Machan

about his sadness.
About how the moon hung full
that morning, every morning

his fist felt like a beast
tethered and tied against its need
to howl and hit and hurt.

About how he needed
the good dope, too, and how she
stared at the gleam in his eyes

with mockery, goddammit, taunts
he wasn't full man enough
to bend the bars of their gray

days, this city of sunless grins.
About how good it felt to take
her pussy, her twat, her tight dark

hole and turn her inside out
like a star (oh, his teacher talked
of similes) and how he hasn't

seen a sky from edge to edge
since somehow he got put in here
where metal clangs and cotton clings

and generous souls who offer classes
have to leave their belts with buckles
behind them at the wordlessly locked door.

"On Learning That My Daughter's Rapist Has Been Taught to Write a Poem" was first published in *Slipstream* (No 36, Fall 2016). Reprinted with permission.

Gravity & Other Forces
Sarah Cooper

We had to let you plummet far and fast – had
to watch your body become wind-burnt

had to watch your life spill over a rocky cliff
plunge into the murky mush, swirl and pool

as a stagnant puddle. We had to let you flail down.
Something should have caught you:

the cliff clipped your skin, the rocks
gnashed against your arms, abrasions

formed, scars settled into your legs. Your body
had to separate from us, had to lay lifeless

before our vivid eyes, gaping mouths and
wordless sobbing. This land of

full body hugs, your son's laughter, mom and dad's smiles
are what you left behind.

Sorry

Zainab Ummer Farook

Your sorries
tumble into one another –
a row of bicycles knocked down
handlebars caught in chains caught in pedals caught in wheels

like the sorry that really is sorry the sorry
that doesn't know whether it's sorry and the sorry
drunk on the belief that a sorry is a Band-Aid

and plasters itself
on all wounds: scraped skin and broken bones,
festering words and fractured promises

a banyan-tree hug
pressing crushing smothering
my despair –
pressing crushing smothering
with antiseptic fury

(sorry)
blazing a trail of nicotine kisses
on parched lips

(sorry)
breathing ethanol-drenched hope
into half-dead dreams

(sorry)
building a pyre of joints
upon which my heart crumbles

into smoke and ash
and the ghosts of all the sorries
you ever said

(I'm sorry.)

Dragon
Katherine DiBella Seluja

on your shoulder
tail non-stop twitching
fire down your gullet all night
iridescent scales float in your head
anything to squelch the fire
hard to focus when the CVS store manager gives you a try
stocking shelves, not too demanding
but so much Cover Girl so much Oil of Olay
so many Crest whitening cotton anklets plastic head bands
tiny teeth run along the edge
bite into your scalp   chew down any thought of sober
how heavy that dragon
how sharp the teeth that finally bled you dry

"Dragon" will be included in the forthcoming book *Gather the Night* by
Katherine Seluja (UNM Press, 2018).

Snow
Katharyn Howd Machan

falls outside my safe brown home
and I am weeping, I am crying:
this house holds two black-striped cats
but God is a distant palace of whim

allowing my daughter to long for a drug
that turns her into thin gray smoke,
vague lips that lie for survival.
Crystals? They're blowing now

swift and silver and silent as hope
only a mother can ask to find
when the body she's birthed and loves
finds heroin is more important

than giving to the wider world
calling out her name. Snow
beautiful and bright and pure
pours down from a streetlit night

here where I dare write a poem
praying that the girl I bore
is able to look out through a window
and wonder at the winter sky.

"Snow" first appeared in *The Healing Muse*. Reprinted with permission.

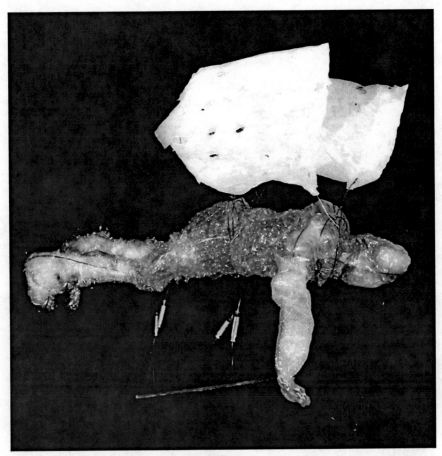

Heroinwhite by Richard Bargdill

Consumed

Sofia L. Taylor

Everything you touch turns to dust.
Instead of happiness, you bring only pain.
You will be the end of me.
No end in sight, no joy left inside.

An illusion, a fantasy, a debt.
A dream, deception, a theft.
Too big to ignore, grandiose to the core.
A nightmare, a spell, a loss.

To surrender is the only hope.
Let go of the promise.
Learn to read between the lines,
And to see the wolf among the sheep.

Self-destruction, denial.
Sabotage and betrayal.
Self-imposed suffering.
One wrong turn, devastated.

Learn to discern, time to move on.
Leave behind the pain,
And find some new terrain.

Separation-Individuation Theory
Marissa Glover

Your wife stands in the kitchen,
hands on her hips, asking again with her eyes
the one question rehab couldn't answer.

So you tell her you were two
and fell down the stairs
and your mom kept watching *Mary Tyler Moore*.

You tell her you were eight,
down by the pond,
and about the frog you stoned to death—
and kept pelting until its guts came out.

You tell her you were twelve,
small for your age,
and how your classmates pushed you
and called you *pussy* when you fell.

Your wife still stands in the kitchen
with her hands on her hips,
and I lie beside you in a cold bed,
covers pulled tight to my chin,
refusing to warm.

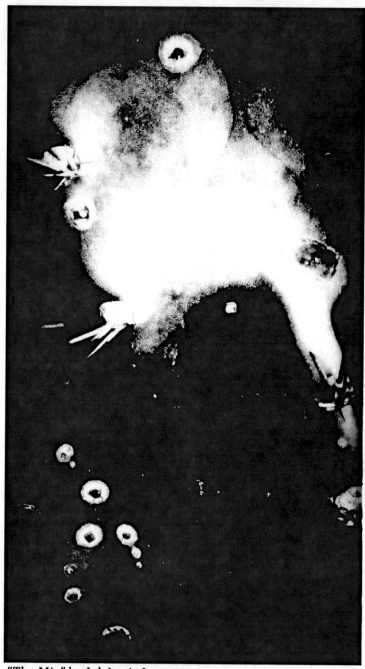

"The Mix" by Jyl Anais Ion

H
Katharyn Howd Machan

Beer makes you fat, whiskey burns,
and marijuana stinks and clings,
so when she went she went straight
to the point, the long one, skinny, silver, sharp
and bright as an enchanted prince's fingers
promising a star-swung dance. *Nothing
makes you feel as good as heroin*
she tells her brother and me as we
bring her heart-shaped foil-wrapped chocolate
for Valentine's Day, snow falling fast.
She's twenty-one; the hard law says
I can't just take her in my arms
and lock her in a warm high tower
with no doorway to the street.
She stares at us and lies again:
she didn't steal four hundred dollars,
she doesn't know why a trooper called,
these cold shadows that were once clear eyes
come from sweet late nights of reading
precious fairy tales.

"H" was previously published in *Blast Furnace*. Reprinted with permission.

Telephone, 4 a.m.
Katherine DiBella Seluja

Wrapped in muslin night

scream of ringing phone,
his stumbling voice gagging

Emergency room, again.

And you think,

What if there were a box to keep him in
somewhere to store him away

to bring out with rainy weather.
Then you'd have time to listen, unravel every line.

You'd be awake already,

sipping vanilla mint tea
your favorite blue glazed mug.

The one with the crack that resembles
the shining scar on his forehead.

How sharp that metal gutter
the night he flew from the roof.

"Telephone, 4 a.m." will be included in the forthcoming book *Gather the Night* by Katherine Seluja (UNM Press, 2018).

Helping Hand
Katrina Lynn Sczesny

I have grown to understand that when it comes to you
there is no helping hand.
You say you care, that you love me,
but all I feel is the betrayal of you letting him
shove me, curse me, hit me, and violate my psyche.
I wonder, at times, if I would have lain there and cried
 instead of standing to fight,
would you have then felt sorry for me?
You talk of sorrow, pain and abuse you endured as a child
and of all that you hold deep inside.
Yet, you let me experience all of the negligence and abuse,
all of the hateful words and violent acts.
You willingly tolerated me crying myself to sleep,
alone and disregarded like trash.
I have excused your inactions and demoralizing words,
but I will no longer be abashed.
While you continue to cleanse yourself in drink
I am freeing my hands of you.
The awe for this mother is gone,
the mother whose love I have not truly known.
I have reared myself to understand
that I do unquestionably have a helping hand.
One of my own.

Relapse
Nicole V. Basta

you call to say
     still alive
     again
     going to die

the stowaways in your body
make plain any pain in mine

i'm just scars cuts scabs birthmarks
those badges to be noted, hardly noticed
just the general stains of how i've grown into myself

you say it again
     going to die
oh well i tried my best oh well

i receive a rattling
applause of how i handle it all
the clappers don't want to handle it at all

you call again, this time from a hospital
     pericarditis
i cannot pronounce it
inflammation of the lining of the heart

you tell me
     this time it's different

because
nitroglycerin will ride home
in your pocket

because
death struck you dumb
in its infection

     never again

the refrain of the last few years
never again

i load you
with distractions
i hang up the phone
to try on my own

i step around the blood
on the sidewalk in chinatown
i crack the spines
of lemons into my glasses

i daydream of whose hand i will hold
at your funeral

for me the sugar in my liquor
is almost always enough

Delirium Tremens

Katherine DiBella Seluja

Let the glass sweat and bleed,
let the foam run dry,

walk away from the drink
and let the shaking begin.

Turn to the buzzing in your head,
flies at an oozing wound

canyons scream at your feet.
Hold tight to that wad of sheets heaving

at the edge of the bed,
your bed is a boat and it's swaying,

swinging to a reggae beat
and the ants just won't stop crawling,

treading down your arm,
a track for the beetles to follow.

Last night you must have killed twenty,

snapping crack of blue green carapace
beneath your trembling feet.

"Delirium Tremens" will be included in the forthcoming book *Gather the Night* by Katherine Seluja (UNM Press, 2018).

Madness

Carolina Borens

... tick ... The tock ... The tick ... The tock ...

It's happening again, time keeps on beating.
You've abandoned me in your darkness.
I feel chaffed by your grit, the ruinous choices
you've made, the outcasts you favored.
My nightmare begins
as I imagine the worst.

Your best friend's a bottle. Your partners are pills.
Your lessons are flurried. Your mind's losing sight.
Your rambling is loose. You don't make any sense.
You don't hear what you say, don't see
what you're doing. My frightened reminders
make you move one step farther. I beg you to stop.
I call who I can. I am reminded once again,
I can't save you from yourself.

I sit near the phone. I watch for signs.
I know when I look back my heart will pull
the blind. I don't want to deal with this.
It's painful to watch. The revolving door spins.
Another beginning is botched.

It's a sickness I scream at the ghost haunting me.
Are you wanting to die? Is it me you want dead?
There are people who love you. Can you please try?
You're hurting. We're hurting. It's all the same kind.
We choose you, beg you to fight for your mind.

... The tick ... The tock ... The tick ...

So the minutes keep passing.
My prayers are for you.
How deep is rock bottom?
Will death meet you there?

I wait for a miracle, the first step of the ten.
I hope for a beginning. I pray for an end.

I look at the clock. Another hour has passed.
I make a few calls. My heart beats too fast.
I have to move forward. There are tasks I must do.
There are others who need me. If only I knew.

I agonize, not knowing if you're alive or dead.
Broken bones. Overdose. Under arrest.
I don't feel it's over. I'm not sensing that dread.
But the heart sometimes lies when the pain
is too much. I'm dizzy from thinking.
Sirens roar, my body stands frozen.
Have you caved to your demons?
Is your fate all but chosen?
Bad news travels fast.
The phone is not ringing.

Before time runs out and the quiet stands still,
in my pitiful plight, I plead for another chance . . .

The tock . . .

The phone rings.
It's you.

The . . .

How Not to Write a Poem

Katharyn Howd Machan

Allow a loved one's illness
to get in the way of your pen
or keyboard or stick in the sand
or even the voice that calls in
your dreams bellowing villanelles.
Say it's your daughter. Say she's

twenty-two and addicted to dope
so you can't do a god-blessed
thing because she's a legal adult.
Go to Al-Anon, live the Twelve Steps,
whittle your guilt to a small
tight splinter and flick it into

hot flames. The places where you keep
your stanzas will disappear in dust.
Vaguely you'll remember needing
enjambment, metaphors, rhyme—
but they're all forgotten now.
You just don't have the time.

"How Not to Write a Poem" was originally published in *H* (Gribble Press, 2014). Reprinted with permission.

Letter to a Friend

Louis Hoffman

For a friend

I see you, brother
With razor blades beneath your skin
Tick, tick, ticking away
You try to wear your skin thick
Yet the scars rising from within
Betray you
Pushing through the sedation
Grasping the surface

On life's stage
We laugh a good laugh
that covers your pain
and disguises my yearning to know
the wounds,
to provide the sacred ointment
of listening over tears
Instead, in weakness,
we laugh

I hope you know, brother,
my love
I hope you forgive
my omission of courage
And, through our shared failures,
I hope you know
that I see you, brother
I see you

About the Editors

Nathaniel Granger, Jr., PsyD, is the founder and director/ psychotherapist at Be REAL Ministries, Inc. in Colorado Springs, Colorado. He tirelessly devotes time to working with homeless and disenfranchised populations, and is the current secretary of the American Psychological Association Society of Humanistic Psychology, and, most recently, its president-elect. He is also a board member of the Rocky Mountain Humanistic Counseling and Psychological Association, where he serves as treasurer. He also serves on the Diversity Taskforce of the National Association of Poetry Therapy. Additionally, he is an adjunct psychology professor at Pikes Peaks Community College in Colorado Springs, Colorado and at Saybrook University in Oakland, California. He is a published author and is particularly passionate about *Silent Screams: Poetic Journeys of Addiction and Recovery. In vivo* experiences, interests in civil rights, and a love for God and humanity form the substrata upon which a majority of his work in academia, writing, and public speaking is predicated. Dr. Granger's family is the catalyst for his humanitarianism and the wind beneath his wings.

Louis Hoffman, PhD, is a psychologist in private practice and a faculty member at Saybrook University. *Silent Screams* is his thirteenth book, and sixth book in the Poetry, Healing, and Growth Series, which helps fulfill a lifelong dream to be an author and poet. He has also published numerous journal articles and book chapters, and serves on the editorial board for several journals. He is a past president of the Society for Humanistic Psychology and is currently the president of the Rocky Mountain Humanistic Counseling and Psychological Association. Dr. Hoffman has been recognized as a fellow of the American Psychological Association (APA), the Society for Humanistic Psychology, the Society for the Study of Aesthetics, Creativity, and the Arts, and APA Division 52 (International Psychology). He serves on the board of The Humanitarian Alliance, the Coalition for Compassion and Action, and the International Institute for Existential-Humanistic Psychology. Most importantly, he is a husband, father, and avid dog lover residing in the beautiful mountains of Colorado.